Here's all the great literature in this grade level of *Celebrate Reading!*

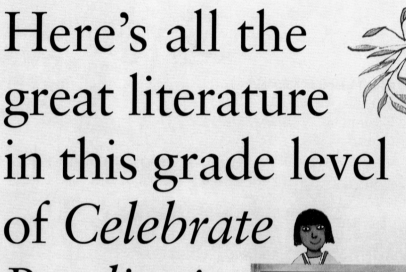

BOOK A
Pig Tales
Stories That Twist

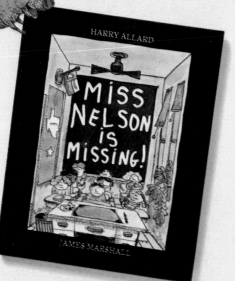
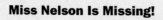

Featured Poets

Jack Prelutsky
Arnold Lobel

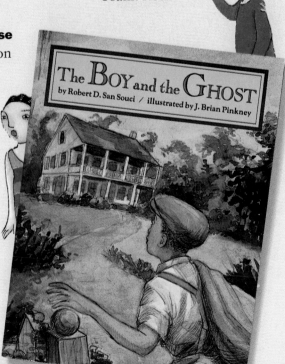

The Boy and the Ghost
by Robert D. San Souci / illustrated by J. Brian Pinkney

BOOK C

How Many Toes Does a Fish Have?

Looking Beneath the Surface

Featured Poet

Joan W. Blos

BOOK E

Dinner with Aliens

and Other Unexpected Situations

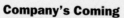

Featured Poet

Lucille Clifton

BOOK F

In Your Wildest Dreams

Imagination at Work

Featured Poets

A. A. Milne
Bill Peet

Celebrate Reading!
Trade Book Library

The Cactus Flower Bakery
by Harry Allard
✳ CHILDREN'S CHOICE AUTHOR

Play Ball, Amelia Bedelia
by Peggy Parish

Fables
by Arnold Lobel
✳ CALDECOTT MEDAL
✳ ALA NOTABLE BOOK

What's Cooking, Jenny Archer?
by Ellen Conford
✳ PARENTS' CHOICE AUTHOR

**She Come Bringing Me
That Little Baby Girl**
by Eloise Greenfield
✳ IRMA SIMONTON BLACK AWARD
✳ BOSTON GLOBE-HORN BOOK
   ILLUSTRATION HONOR
✳ CHILDREN'S CHOICE

The Show-and-Tell War
by Janice Lee Smith
✳ CHILDREN'S CHOICE
✳ *SCHOOL LIBRARY JOURNAL* BEST BOOK

King of the Birds
by Shirley Climo
✳ NOTABLE SOCIAL STUDIES TRADE BOOK

Fossils Tell of Long Ago
by Aliki
✳ LIBRARY OF CONGRESS
   CHILDREN'S BOOK
✳ OUTSTANDING SCIENCE TRADE BOOK

Willie's Not the Hugging Kind
by Joyce Durham Barrett

The Paper Crane
by Molly Bang
✳ ALA NOTABLE CHILDREN'S BOOK
✳ BOSTON GLOBE-HORN BOOK AWARD
✳ *SCHOOL LIBRARY JOURNAL* BEST BOOK
✳ READING RAINBOW SELECTION

Don't Tell the Whole World
by Joanna Cole
✳ CHILDREN'S CHOICE AUTHOR

**The Spooky Tail of
Prewitt Peacock**
by Bill Peet
✳ CHILDREN'S CHOICE AUTHOR

Dinner
WITH ALIENS

AND OTHER UNEXPECTED SITUATIONS

About the Cover Artist
Flora Jew has lived in California all her lfie. She started to draw in kindergarten and hasn't stopped since. She loves to illustrate books for children and is amazed that she can earn a living doing what comes so easily. It doesn't even seem like work! Flora likes to move fast, so skiing is her favorite sport. She lives near San Francisco with her husband and two sons.

ISBN: 0-673-81143-3

1997
Scott, Foresman and Company, Glenview, Illinois
All Rights Reserved.
Printed in the United States of America.

Acknowledgments appear on page 128.

2345678910DQ010099989796

Dinner WITH ALIENS

AND OTHER UNEXPECTED SITUATIONS

ScottForesman

A Division of HarperCollinsPublishers

Contents

Changing Places
Genre Study

The Ghost of

by Suzy Kline

illustrations by the third-graders at Pritzker School and
LaSalle Language Academy, Chicago, Illinois

Annabelle

Herbie Jones rang the doorbell.

He didn't want to be the one to do this, but his third-grade teacher, Miss Pinkham, said he had to because he lived around the corner. Margie Sherman was supposed to do it, but she was sent home from school with a fever.

Herbie looked at the Siamese cat sitting on the porch. He didn't look very friendly.

Herbie rang the doorbell again.

A tall, thin man with glasses answered. "Why hello, Herbie."

"Hello, Mr. Hodgekiss. I brought Annabelle some Get Well cards from our class. Here. Would you please give them to her?" Herbie figured he had done his job so he turned around and headed down the steps.

"Just a minute, Herbie. Won't you come in and give the cards to Annabelle yourself? The doctor said she isn't contagious anymore."

Herbie stopped cold.

He was just supposed to deliver them to the door.

Not go in.

Miss Pinkham never said he had to do that.

Anyway, he and Annabelle Louisa Hodgekiss weren't even talking to each other.

Ever since the poster contest for Mr. D's Card Shop in town, Annabelle had decided not to talk to anyone in the class who didn't raise their hand for her daisy poster. Herbie had voted for his best friend Raymond Martin's poster, the one with the Viking ship.

Herbie remembered how quickly Annabelle took out her memo cube with her initials ALH on it and recorded names. His name was the first one on the list, AND it had three checks after it.

"Just for a minute?" Mr. Hodgekiss repeated.

Herbie was trapped. He half nodded and walked into the house. He felt his throat getting dry and raspy.

Herbie sure didn't like going into a girl's bedroom. His sister's was barricaded with signs like DO NOT ENTER!, DO NOT DISTURB!, GENIUS AT WORK!, and BEWARE OF DOG! Herbie thought the last sign was dumb. They didn't have a dog.

When he got to Annabelle's door, he noticed how clean and white it was. There wasn't even one poster tacked on it.

Mr. Hodgekiss turned to Herbie. "Before we go in, I must tell you something. Annabelle has been very stubborn about having the chicken pox."

Herbie's answer squeaked like a frog. "Reaaally?" He tried to act surprised, but the fact was, Herbie already knew Annabelle was stubborn—about everything.

Mr. Hodgekiss took his glasses off and wiped them with a crisp white handkerchief. "She insists on putting her sheet over her head every time someone other than her mother goes into her room. She won't even let ME see her

face. She says when the spots and scabs are gone in a few days, she won't hide behind the sheet."

"No kidding?" Herbie replied. He liked the idea of visiting someone with a sheet over her head. It was like visiting a ghost—the ghost of Annabelle. "When is she coming back to school?" Herbie hoped she'd wear her sheet to class.

"Friday. I guess there is something important going on that day at school."

"Oh, yeah..." Herbie mumbled, half listening. He was still picturing what it would be like to sit next to a ghost in class. It was a neat idea, he thought.

"Well...maybe you'll have better luck with her," Mr. Hodgekiss continued. Then he knocked on Annabelle's door. "Dear, may we come in?"

"Who's with you?"

"Someone from school. He has some Get Well cards for you." Mr. Hodgekiss opened the door slowly.

Herbie saw Annabelle sitting up in bed. The sheet was tucked behind her head.

"Who is it?" she asked again.

Mr. Hodgekiss bent over and picked some green lint off the bedroom carpet. "See for yourself, dear." Then he walked out, smiling at Herbie.

Herbie quickly looked around the room. He noticed the daisy poster hanging on the wall. The blue ribbon was still on it.

Herbie sat down at Annabelle's desk. He felt a tickle in his throat, "Hi...hi, Annabelle."

"Do you have a cold, John, or is that your asthma acting up again?"

John?

Hey, this could be fun, Herbie thought. Here he was visiting a ghost, and now he could even pretend he was someone else. "Just . . . just my asthma," Herbie replied, clearing his voice. He decided not to say too much. He didn't want to spoil the game.

"Did you bring me some cards?"

"Yup." Herbie looked at Annabelle. He could barely make out her nose and eye sockets, but when she said something, the sheet puffed out from her lips. Herbie thought she made kind of a cute ghost, if you could call a girl cute.

"Here's two," Herbie said, pulling them out of a manila folder.

"Read them to me," Annabelle asked.

"Sure," Herbie said as he placed the folder on her bookcase. He noticed the books were arranged alphabetically by author, and that they were all chapter books.

"Here's one with a Viking ship on it."

"I know, that's from Raymond Martin. He always draws Viking ships."

"Yup, and on the inside it says, BON VOYAGE!"

"BON VOYAGE?" The sheet billowed around her lips.

Herbie remembered seeing those words on cards at Mr. D's. The cards were Ray's favorites because they had ships and planes on them.

Annabelle shook her head. "That's dumb. *Bon voyage* means have a good trip. Having the chicken pox is NOT having fun, and you certainly can't go anywhere!"

Herbie shrugged. He thought staying out of school for a week would be fun. Then he remembered to cough a few times and act like John.

"Here's a real nice card. It has you in bed with your cat and a thermometer in your mouth."

"Hmm, I wonder who made that one?"

"It even has a poem inside." Herbie began reading:

> Annabelle, Annabelle,
>   sick in bed
> Spots on her nose
> And spots on her head
> Think I will give her a
>   brite red rose
> Then she nos
>   I will tickel her toes
> With it.

Annabelle giggled so much her sheet shook. "That's funny! Who wrote it?"

Herbie tipped back his chair: "Herbie Jones."

Annabelle straightened up. "Herbie Jones wrote THAT?"

"The one and only," Herbie said proudly.

Annabelle was quiet for a moment. Then her cat, Sukey, jumped up on the bed, and she started petting his fur. "Well . . . you know, John."

"Yes, Annabelle . . ." Herbie was enjoying this.

"I'm not speaking to Herbie . . ."

"Uh huh . . ."

"And it's not just because he didn't vote for my daisy poster."

"Oh?" Herbie wondered if he was going to find out why his name had three checks after it.

"Herbie Jones wore earrings to school in October!"

Herbie counted one check to himself.

"It was Halloween," Annabelle continued, "and he was supposed to be a pirate. Everyone knows a pirate wears just one *gold* earring. Herbie wore a pair of strawberries."

Herbie remembered. It was the first pair he found. He didn't want to hang around his sister's room for too long. She'd kill him for getting into her jewelry.

". . . and," Annabelle went on, "he wrote a story at Thanksgiving time about a turkey who got his head chopped off, and he called the turkey Annabelle."

Herbie grinned. The story was one of his favorites. That was check two, he figured.

". . . and he gave me a can of salmon for my birthday."

Check three. What a memory, Herbie thought. He decided to leave. It was getting dangerous. He figured he had played John long enough.

"But," Annabelle added as she smoothed her sheet, "Herbie Jones does have a way with words."

Herbie stopped at the door. "Herbie Jones has a way with words?"

"IF YOU TELL HERBIE I SAID THAT, JOHN GREENWEED, I'LL KILL YOU!"

Herbie snatched a Kleenex from the flowered box on her desk and held it up to his mouth. This was no time to be discovered now. "I won't," Herbie said, talking into the tissue. "Your secret is safe with me."

Mr. Hodgekiss saw Herbie to the door. "Did she talk to you face to face?"

"No," Herbie said, feeling somewhat guilty. "She even thinks . . . I'm . . . John Greenweed. I kind of went along with it . . . in fun."

Herbie wondered if he was going to get in trouble.

"Listen, Herbie, if my daughter wants to play games, other people can too. Your secret is safe with me, *John*." He winked.

Herbie smiled. He was glad Mr. Hodgekiss had a sense of humor.

As Herbie shuffled along the sidewalk, he kept thinking about what Annabelle had said: "Herbie Jones does have a way with words."

Thinking About It

1

When you are sick, how do you feel about seeing your friends? What makes you feel better?

2

Herbie lets Annabelle think he is someone else. Why does he do that? Was it a good idea? Why?

3

Annabelle wants to hide her chicken pox, so she covers her head with a sheet. What else could she do?

The Life of Herbie Jones Continues . . .

Herbie, a bank robber, and a flea-bitten dog will all remember Herbie's summer after third grade in *Herbie Jones and the Hamburger Head* by Suzy Kline.

COMPANY'S COMING

by Arthur Yorinks
illustrations by David Small

On the day Shirley had invited all of her relatives
to dinner and Moe, her husband, was pleasantly
tinkering in the yard, a flying saucer quietly landed next
to their toolshed. Moe was surprised.

"Shirley!" he yelled.

Shirley joined Moe on the patio.

"Moe, you had to buy *that* barbecue? It's too big,"
she complained.

"Shirl, it's not a barbecue," Moe said.

Suddenly, a small hatch on the saucer opened and out walked two visitors from outer space.

"Greetings," they spoke in English. "We come in peace. Do you have a bathroom?"

Stunned, Shirley replied, "Down the hall and to the left." The foreigners nodded graciously and walked into the house.

"How could you let them into our house!" Moe was upset.

"Did you see those helmets? Those ray guns? They'll vaporize us!" Moe was very upset.

"Shhush, they're coming," Shirley whispered. "Stay calm. Be polite. Maybe we can make friends with them."

"What a lovely house you have," the strangers commented. "What do you call this place?"

"Bellmore," Shirley politely answered. The visitors nodded.

"We're from away. Far away. And we've been traveling for years on our way to the next galaxy—"

"How about a sandwich, you must be hungry," Shirley nervously interrupted. "Would you like to stay for dinner?"

"Gee!" they replied. "We'd love to. We'll return at six o'clock." The spacemen went back to their ship and flew off. Moe and Shirley ran into the house.

"Are you crazy! The cousins are coming tonight. Why did you invite *them* to dinner?" Moe asked. "They'll atomize us. Bellmore . . . the whole Earth is doomed, I tell you!" Moe was hysterical.

"Moe, Moe, take it easy. They look like nice boys,"
Shirley said. "Come, help me make the potato salad."

But Moe had other thoughts. Saying he had to wash
his hands, he went upstairs and called the FBI. The FBI
called the Pentagon. And the Pentagon called the Army,
the Air Force, and the Marines.

At a quarter to six, the house was
surrounded.

Inside, the cousins sat, panicked.

"Act natural," Shirley told her relatives. "Be nice. So they look a little different, I'm sure they're friendly," she said, as she served the appetizers.

"Don't worry," Moe added. "If those aliens make one false move, they've had it! So relax."

Moe heard a humming and ran to the window. "They're here!" he yelled.

The doorbell rang. Everyone froze. Cousin Etta fainted.

"I'll get it," Shirley called. She went to the door. "Hello, hello, come right in," she greeted the men from outer space. They were carrying a box.

"How about a drink, some soda? Are you tired? It's getting late, if you leave now you'll just miss the traffic." Moe tried to usher them out.

"So, guys, what's new, have you been to Venus yet, I hear it's hot in the summer," Cousin Sheldon the loudmouth asked. The spacemen sat.

"Well, we're on our way to check out a new planet. Our population has grown so quickly that we must branch out and find new places to live; know what I mean?"

"Sure, we know what you mean," Moe blurted out. "An invasion—we're doomed," he whispered to Cousin Harriet.

"Dinner!" Shirley called.

"Oh, please, before dinner, we have something for you. It'll knock you out." The visitors presented their box.

"It's a bomb! It's gas! It's a laser!" Etta yelled and then fainted again. Soldiers burst into the house. Tanks pointed their guns.

Shirley gingerly began to unwrap the gift. "We weren't sure if you had one of these," the men started to say.

Shirley interrupted. "It's a, it's a, it's a—"
The cousins were paralyzed.

"It's a, it's a," Shirley continued. Moe was sweating from head to foot. "OH!" Shirley blurted. Etta, Moe, and Sheldon fainted.

"It's a *blender!*" Shirley declared.
"And we don't even have one."

"We thought you'd like it. And it was on sale!" The spacemen beamed. Shirley went over and kissed them both. "Let's eat!" she said.

Luckily, Shirley had made extra spaghetti and meatballs. The cousins, the soldiers, the pilots, the Marines, the FBI men—everyone sat down and had a delicious meal; from soup to nuts.

thinking
about it

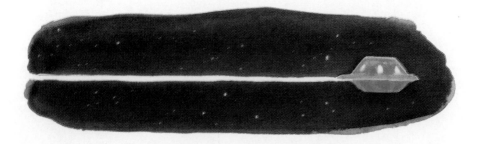

1 The aliens have just landed where you live! What will you do? What will your family do?

2 The creatures from outer space sure look different, but are they really? How are they like people? How are they different?

3 The aliens invite Moe and Shirley to dinner on their planet. What is their planet like? What do they serve for dinner? What can Moe and Shirley bring as a gift?

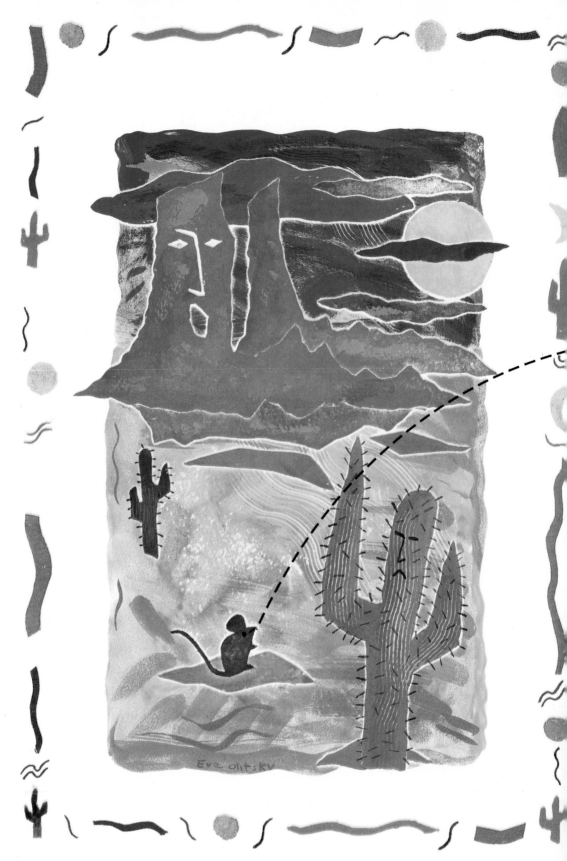

Eva Olitsky

Kan Kan *can*

by Carmen Tafolla

Kan Kan was a little kangaroo rat that lived in the desert. Kan Kan liked to jump very high and travel very far. Like most kangaroo rats, Kan Kan ate seeds and nuts and got his water from chewing on juicy leaves or little berries. In fact, Kan Kan never had to drink water at all! Kan Kan was tiny but very, very remarkable.

One day when Kan Kan had jumped very high and traveled very far, he heard a giant voice rumble, "Oh, how magnificent am I, for who in all the world can survive on less water than I?"

It was the desert who was speaking. And it spoke to the cactus. Now cacti are known for being very grumpy, but they are also very honest. "Hmph!" said the cactus.

"Don't be jealous, Cactus, just because I'm more magnificent than you. Tell me honestly, who in all the world can survive on less water than I?"

And the cactus answered, "Kan Kan can."

"Why, how can that be?" quaked the desert.

The cactus explained. "When every once in a blue moon the skies rain in the desert, who drinks their water? You do. Yet Kan Kan, the tiny kangaroo rat, drinks no water ever. All his liquid comes from juicy leaves or berries, and never once has he drunk a drop of water."

"You are right," said the desert. "What a magnificent creature Kan Kan must be."

The mountain overheard their conversation and in its high and shivery voice, it bragged, "Oh, how magnificent am *I*, for who in all the world can rise higher than I?"

And the grumpy old cactus sighed, "Kan Kan can."

"Why, how can that be?" asked the mountain, startled.

And the cactus, a bit tired of so much talking, answered, "For all your height, Mountain, have you ever jumped? No, you are the same height you always are, and never reach any higher than your own height. Yet, Kan Kan, the tiny kangaroo rat, every day reaches many, many times his own height, leaping five, and ten, and even twenty times his own height. In that, he rises much higher than you."

"You are right," said the mountain. "What a magnificent creature Kan Kan must be."

Through all this, the beautiful desert sky was laying its magical evening colors along the horizon, from pinks and oranges, where the sun was just setting, to deep purples and shiny blacks on the opposite end of the desert. And it whispered in its smooth and feathery voice, "Oh, how magnificent am *I*, for who in all the world can go farther than I?"

And the cactus grumbled, "Kan Kan can."

"Why, how can that be?" asked the sky, very shocked.

And the cactus, irritated by all this chatter, said, in a very thorny voice, "You, Sky, for as far as you spread above us, do you ever go anywhere? No.

For whenever we look up to see you, there you are. Still in the same place! Yet Kan Kan, the tiny kangaroo rat, can travel so far that one could search the desert for years and still not find him."

"You are right," said the sky. "What a magnificent creature Kan Kan must be."

And then the desert and the mountain and the sky looked at each other, embarrassed by all their bragging, and looked at tiny Kan Kan, and said, "Oh, how magnificent is Kan Kan, for who in all the world can think of anyone more magnificent than he?"

And a little, tiny, kangaroo-rat voice answered, "Kan Kan can." And then Kan Kan crawled up against the warmth of his little kangaroo-rat mother, and went to sleep. And the desert and the mountain and the sky, and even the cactus, smiled.

Thinking About It

1

The cactus thinks Kan Kan is the most magnificent. What is your favorite animal? Why is it the most magnificent?

2

The author uses special words to describe the voices of the sky, mountain, and other characters. What are some of the special words? What do they tell you about the characters?

3

You're going to do "Kan Kan Can" as a play. How will you make costumes for the sky, mountain, desert, and cactus? How will you create the sounds of their voices? What other special sounds and scenery can you make?

Everett Anderson's
Friend

by Lucille Clifton
illustrations by Gil Ashby

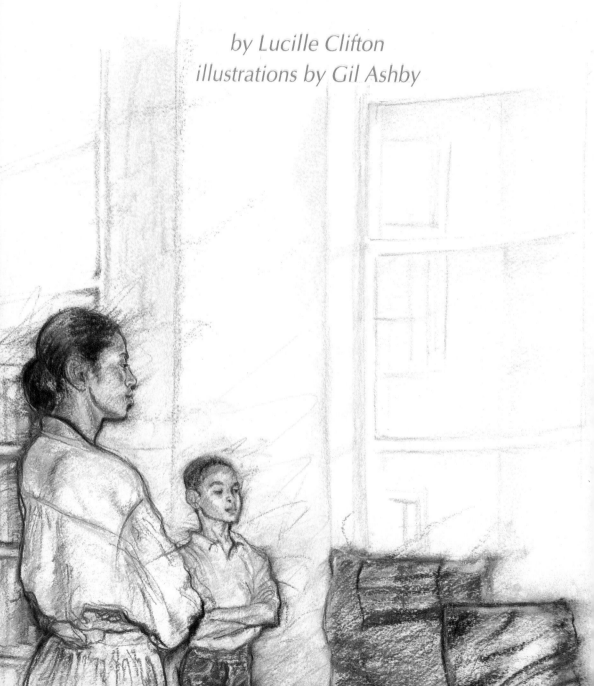

Someone new has come to stay
in 13A, in 13A
and Everett Anderson's Mama and he
can't wait to see, can't wait to see
whether it's girls or
whether it's boys and
how are their books and
how are their toys and
where they've been and
where they go and
who are their friends and
the people they know,
oh, someone new has come to stay
next door in 13A.

If not an almost
brother,
why not something
other
like a bird or
a cat or
a cousin or
a dozen uncles?

Please,
says Everett Anderson softly,
why did they have to be
a family of
shes?

Girls named Maria who
win at ball
are not a bit of fun
at all.
No, girls who can run
are just no fun
thinks Everett Anderson!

In 14A when Mama's at work
sometimes Joe and sometimes Kirk
can come till she gets home and be
Everett Anderson's company.

Three boys are just the right amount
for playing games that count,
there isn't any room, you see,
for girls named Maria in company.

If Daddy was here
he would let me in and
call me a careless boy
and then
(even though I
forgot my key)
he would make peanut butter
and jelly for me,
and not be mad
and I'd be glad.

If Daddy was here
he could let me in
thinks Everett Anderson
again.

45

A girl named Maria
is good to know
when you haven't got
any place to go
and you forgot your
apartment key.

Why, she can say,
"Come in with me,
and play in 13A and wait
if your Mama is working late."

Even if she beats at races it's
nicer to lose in familiar places.

Maria's Mama makes little pies
called *Tacos*,
calls little boys *Muchachos*,
and likes to thank the *Dios*;
oh, 13A is a lovely surprise
to Everett Anderson's eyes!

Everett Anderson's Mama is mad
because he lost the key he had;
but a boy has so many things to do
he can't remember them and keys, too.
And if Daddy were here he would say,
"We'll talk about it another day,"
thinks the boy who got a fussing at
for just a little thing like that.

A girl named Maria
who wins at ball
is fun to play with
after all
and Joe and Kirk and
Maria too
are just the right number
for things to do.

Lose a key,
win a friend,
things have a way of
balancing out,
Everett Anderson's Mama explains,
and that's what the world is all about.

And the friends we find
are full of surprises
Everett Anderson realizes.

Everett Anderson's *Year*

by Lucille Clifton
illustrations by Gil Ashby

February

Everett Anderson
in the snow
is a specially
ice cream boy to know
as he jumps and calls
and spins and falls
with his chocolate nose and
vanilla toes.

April

Rain is good
for washing leaves
and stones and bricks and
even eyes,
and if you hold
your head just so
you can almost see
the tops of skies.

June

In 14A, till Mama comes home
bells are for ringing
and windows for singing
and halls are for skating
and doors are for waiting.

December

" The end of a thing
   is never the end,
   something is always
   being born like
   a year or a baby."

" I don't understand,"
   Everett Anderson says.
" I don't understand where
   the whole thing's at."

" It's just about Love,"
   his Mama smiles.
" It's all about Love and
   you know about that."

53

Everett Anderson's Author

by Lucille Clifton

As a writer, I write about the things I know. All writers do. That's how we are able to make the stories we write and the characters in them seem real. When I wrote *Some of the Days of Everett Anderson*, the first book about Everett, my oldest son was six years old. Since I knew what six-year-old boys were like, that's what I made Everett.

54

I included other things that I know about in my Everett Anderson stories. I have memories from my own childhood. I have my own six children and all their friends to give me inspiration. I know about living in apartments and public housing. I know what not having a lot of money is like, and I know about not having as many things as other kids might have.

But the most important thing that I know is that not having things doesn't mean someone isn't as good as another person. There is nothing wrong with someone if he or she doesn't have as much as someone else. How we feel and how we treat others are things that really matter. Everett Anderson may not have many things, but he has a strong spirit.

I guess it's his strong spirit that makes us care about Everett Anderson and what happens to him. Some characters have lives like ours, and some don't. We come to care about characters, whether they are

like us or not, because we share the same feelings. Our lives may or may not be like Everett Anderson's, but we know and understand Everett because he has some of the same feelings we all have. Feelings don't depend on where we live, what we have, or what kind of family we come from.

I think we learn to understand feelings and we learn to wonder about things by reading. My family were great readers. Neither of my parents graduated from elementary school, but they both loved words. Both my parents read books all the time, so I grew up loving books. The love of words was something that was very natural to me. I grew up reading everything I could get my hands on. I was one of those cereal-box readers.

I still love books. I love what they can say to us.

Thinking
*A*bout It

1 Everett Anderson changed his mind about someone who moved into 13A. When have you changed your mind about someone? What helped you change your mind?

2 What happened to help Everett Anderson change his mind about Maria and her family?

3 A new family is moving into 13C. Be Everett Anderson and show what you'll do this time.

Life with Everett Anderson

Everett Anderson's going to have to look at babies in a new way in *Everett Anderson's Nine Month Long* by Lucille Clifton.

DIGGING UP THE PAST

from *U*S* Kids Magazine*
by Emily M. Schell

The kids dig up dirt and put it into a bucket. Then they pour the dirt through a special net, which is made of wire.

Think about the place where you live. Do you ever wonder who lived there 1,000 years ago?

Some kids at McLeod School in Montana wondered about that. And they decided to look for some answers. They grabbed some tools and went digging.

Went digging? Yep! That's what they did.

The kids started digging on a plot of dirt near their school. They found pieces of glass, wire, and a lid to a jar. A scientist who was on the dig with the kids says these things are about 100 years old. American settlers might have left them there.

Dirt passes through the net, but larger things stay on top.

The kids dug deeper. They found bones from a deer. The bones had been buried for many years.

The kids dug even deeper. They found rocks that had been brought from many miles away. The rocks might have been used around campfires hundreds of years ago. People often place rocks in a circle to keep fire from spreading.

One kid found a piece of pottery made by Shoshone Indians. The scientist says this piece is almost 1,000 years old!

Other kids found some old tools. The tools might have been used by Indians who once lived there.

The glass, wire, lid, bones, rocks, pottery piece, and tools helped answer questions the kids had before they began digging.

Some people who live in the town of McLeod want to put these things in a museum. The things will help many people answer questions they have about the past.

Pieces of glass, a jar lid, and pieces of Indian pottery are some of the things the kids dug up.

The House on

MAPLE
STREET

by Bonnie Pryor

This is 107 Maple Street. Chrissy and Jenny live here with their mother and father, a dog named Maggie, and a fat cat named Sally.

Three hundred years ago there was no house here or even a street. There was only a forest and a bubbling spring where the animals came to drink.

One day a fierce storm roared across the forest. The sky rolled with thunder, and lightning crashed into a tree. A deer sniffed the air in alarm. Soon the woods were ablaze.

The next spring a few sturdy flowers poked through the ashes, and by the year after that the land was covered with grass. Some wildflowers grew at the edge of the stream where the deer had returned to drink.

One day the earth trembled, and a cloud of dust rose to the sky. A mighty herd of buffalo had come to eat the sweet grass and drink from the stream.

People came, following the buffalo herd. They set up
their tepees near the stream, and because they liked it so
much, they stayed for the whole summer.

One boy longed to be a great hunter like his father, but
for now he could only pretend with his friends. In their
games, one boy was chosen to be the buffalo.

His father taught the boy how to make an arrowhead and
smooth it just so, the way his father had taught him. But the
boy was young, and the day was hot.

He ran off to play with his friends and left the
arrowhead on a rock. When he came back later to get it,
he could not find it.

The buffalo moved on, searching for new grass, and the people packed up their tepees and followed.

For a long time the land was quiet. Some rabbits made their home in the stump of a burned tree, and a fox made a den in some rocks.

One day there was a new sound. The fox looked up. A wagon train passed by, heading for California. The settlers stopped beside the stream for a night. But they dreamed of gold and places far away and were gone the next morning.

Other wagons came, following the tracks of the first. The fox family moved into the woods, but the rabbits stayed snug in their burrows until the people had gone.

Soon after, a man and a woman camped along the stream. They were heading west, but the woman would soon have a child. They looked around them and knew it was a good place to stay. The man cut down trees and made a house.

He pulled up the tree stumps left from the fire and planted his crops. The child was a girl, and they named her Ruby and called her their little jewel.

Ruby had a set of china dishes that she played with every day. One day when she was making a mudpie on the banks of the stream, she found an arrowhead buried deep in the ground. She put it in a cup to show her father when he came in from the fields.

Ruby's mother called her to watch the new baby. While she was gone, a rabbit sniffed at the cup and knocked it off the rock. It fell into the tunnel to his burrow, and the rabbit moved away to a new home under the roots of a tree.

Ruby grew up and moved away, but her brother stayed on the farm. By now there were other people nearby, and he married a girl from another farm. They had six children, and he built a larger house so they would all fit.

Now the old wagon trail was used as a road, and the dust got into the house. When his wife complained, Ruby's brother planted a row of maple trees along the road to keep out the dust and shade the house. After the children were grown, he and his wife moved away, but one of their daughters stayed on the farm with her husband and children.

One day the children's great-aunt Ruby came for a visit. She was an old lady with snow-white hair. The children loved to hear her stories of long ago. She told them about the cup and arrowhead she had lost when she was a girl.

After she left, the children looked and looked. But they never found them, though they searched for days.

The town had grown nearly to the edge of the farm, and another man up the road filled in the stream and changed its course. For a while there was a trickle of water in the spring when the snow melted, but weeds and dirt filled in the bed, until hardly anyone remembered a stream had ever been there.

New people lived on the farm. It was the schoolteacher and his family, and they sold much of the land to others. The road was paved with bricks, so there was no longer any dust, but the maple trees remained. The branches hung down over the road, making it shady and cool. People called it Maple Street. Automobiles drove on the road, along with carts and wagons, and there were many new houses.

The house was crumbling and old, and one day some
men tore it down. For a while again, the land was bare. The
rabbits lived comfortably, with only an occasional owl or
fox to chase them. But one day a young couple came
walking along and stopped to admire the trees.

"What a wonderful place for a home," said the young
woman. So they hired carpenters and masons to build a
cozy house of red bricks with white trim.

The young couple lived happily in the house for several
years. The young man got a job in another town, and they
had to move.

The house was sold to a man and a woman who had two girls named Chrissy and Jenny and a dog named Maggie, and a fat cat named Sally.

The girls helped their father dig up a spot of ground for a garden, but it was Maggie the dog who dug up something white in the soft spring earth.

"Stop," cried Chrissy, and she picked up the tiny cup made of china. Inside was the arrowhead found and lost so long ago.

"Who lost these?" the girls wondered. Chrissy and Jenny put the cup and arrowhead on a shelf for others to see. Someday perhaps their children will play with the tiny treasures and wonder about them, too. But the cup and arrowhead will forever keep their secrets, and the children can only dream.

THINKING
About It

1 The place where the house sits has changed many times. Which time would you like to visit? Show the picture you'd step into. Tell what you'd do.

2 "Who lost these?" Chrissy and Jenny wondered. What would you tell them about the cup and the arrowhead?

3 It's 100 years in the future. What is there in place of your home? What could someone find that would show that you once lived there? What would that person say? What would he or she do with it?

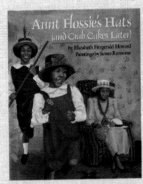

DISCOVERING OUR PAST
Each of Aunt Flossie's hats has a story. Susan and Sarah never tire of hearing them all in *Aunt Flossie's Hats (and Crab Cakes Later)* by Elizabeth Fitzgerald Howard.

How to DIG A HOLE to the Other Side of the World

by Faith McNulty

Find a soft place.
Take a shovel
and start to dig a hole.
The dirt you dig up is called loam.
Loam, or topsoil, is made up of
tiny bits of rock
mixed with many other things,
such as plants and worms that died
and rotted long ago.
When you have dug
through the topsoil
you will come to clay or gravel or sand.
The digging will be harder.

When the hole is five or six feet deep,
you had better ask a friend to help.
He can pull up the clay or gravel
in a bucket,
while you stay at the bottom of the hole
and keep digging.
Sooner or later you will come to rocks;
all sorts of rocks; big rocks, little rocks;
granite, limestone, sandstone.
If you started your hole in Africa
you might find diamonds.
In Brazil you might find emeralds.
In other places you might find coal—
or gold or silver.

START

Wherever you dig watch for
old bones and shells.
The bones of many animals—
dinosaurs, giant tigers, turtles,
and other creatures of long ago—
are buried everywhere.
If you find some, dust them off carefully and
save them.

When you have dug about fifty feet down—
maybe more or maybe less—
you will come to solid rock.
This is the rocky skin of the earth,
called the crust. It is mostly granite.
To dig through it you will need
a drilling machine.
Start drilling.

FOSSIL VERY OLD

You may hit water.
Rain sinks through the topsoil
and gathers in pools
and underground rivers.
If you come to water you should put on
a diving suit.
You may come to a lake of black, gooey oil.
If you hit oil it would be best
to give up this hole and start another
somewhere else.
Keep drilling.

OIL

UNDERGROUND

1 MILE
5280 FT
1.6 KILOMETERS

GEYSER

When you have drilled down a mile
or so, the rock will be warm.
This is because heat flows up into the rock
from the center of the earth.
You may hit boiling water or steam.
This is because rainwater drips down
through cracks onto very hot rock.
Sometimes it comes up again.
In some places on earth, hot water
bubbles up in springs,
or shoots up in geysers.
Because of the boiling water and steam
you will need an asbestos diving suit.
Stay out of the way of geysers.

If you got caught in a geyser it might
carry you up to the surface and shoot you
into the air. When you came down,
you would have to start digging all over again.

Keep drilling for ten or twenty miles.
You will come to a kind of rock called basalt.
Basalt is black and hard
and smooth and heavy.
There is a layer of basalt two or three miles
thick wrapped around the earth.
Keep drilling.
As you go deeper the basalt will get
hotter and hotter.

10Mi.

20Mi.
BASALT

It will get so hot that it will melt
and glow dark red.
Melted basalt is called magma.
This is the stuff that sometimes
shoots out of cracks in the earth
and makes volcanoes. When it cools
on top of the ground, it is called lava.
Volcanoes are very dangerous.
Be careful and don't get caught in one.

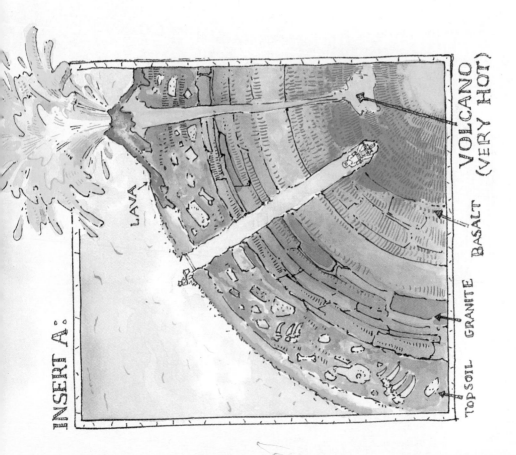

INSERT A:

LAVA

TOPSOIL   GRANITE   BASALT   VOLCANO
(VERY HOT)

To go through red-hot magma you will need
a jet-propelled submarine.
It must have a super
cooling system,
a fireproof skin and a drill
at the tip of its nose.
Your no-spaceship must be very strong.
An ordinary one would be squashed by the
weight of the magma around it.
Or burned up by the heat.

MAGMA
(MELTED BASALT)

INSERT B: FIREPROOF-NO-SPACESHIP

HATCH
PORT WINDOW
PERISCOPE
AIR CONDITIONER
DRILL BIT
STORAGE
KEEL
PROPELLER
RUDDER
AIRHOSE

SCALE 1 2 3 4 5
5 CM = 1 M

Down here below the crust of the earth
it is hotter than any fire you ever felt.
And it will get hotter and hotter
the deeper you go.
When you have gone down about
a hundred and fifty miles,
you are in what is called
the mantle of the earth.
The mantle is made of basalt that
is melted into goo and at the same
time is harder than steel.
It is melted by the great heat
and is hard because of the great weight above
pressing it down.
Keep drilling.

150 Mi.
MANTLE

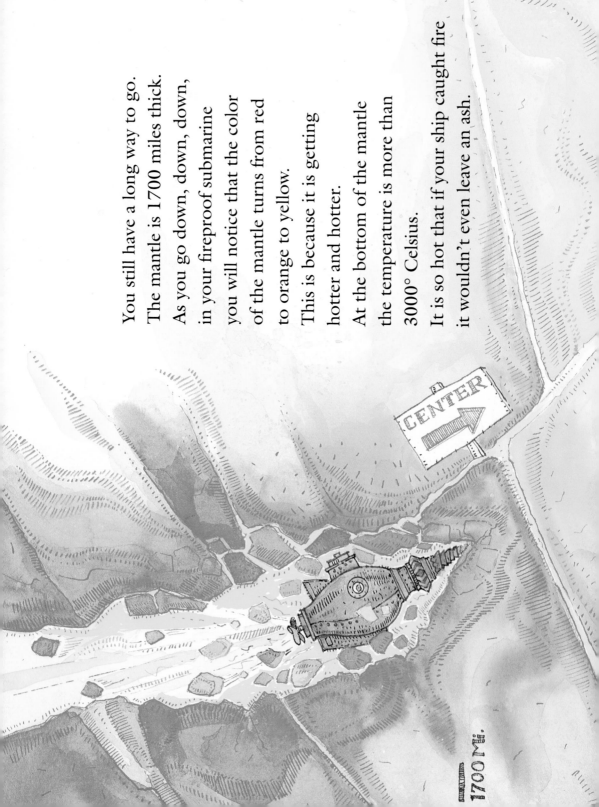

You still have a long way to go.
The mantle is 1700 miles thick.
As you go down, down, down,
in your fireproof submarine
you will notice that the color
of the mantle turns from red
to orange to yellow.
This is because it is getting
hotter and hotter.
At the bottom of the mantle
the temperature is more than
3000° Celsius.
It is so hot that if your ship caught fire
it wouldn't even leave an ash.

CENTER

1700 Mi.

At the bottom of the mantle
you are more than halfway
to the center of the earth.
Now you must go through what is
called the outer core of the earth.
It is a mixture of melted rock and iron.
It is 1300 miles thick.
It will be hard going, but if you
have come this far you should keep on.
You are getting very close
to the center of the earth.

1800 mi.
OUTER CORE

89

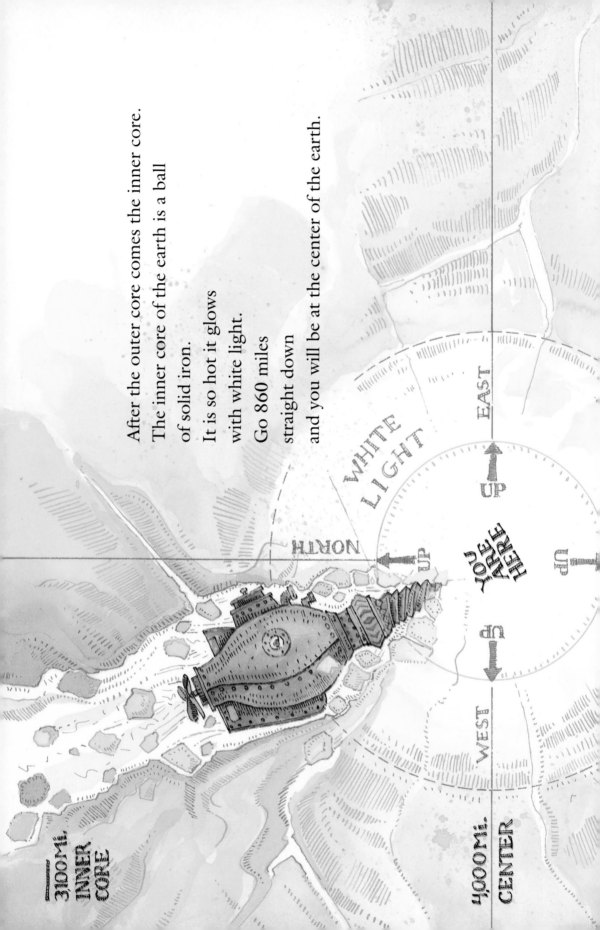

After the outer core comes the inner core.

The inner core of the earth is a ball

of solid iron.

It is so hot it glows

with white light.

Go 860 miles

straight down

and you will be at the center of the earth.

WHITE LIGHT

NORTH

EAST

UP

UP

YOU ARE HERE

UP

UP

WEST

3100 mi. INNER CORE

4,000 mi. CENTER

The center of the earth is a place where
east meets west, north meets south,
and up meets down.
At the center of the earth
there is nothing under you.
Every direction is up.
Your feet are pointing up
and your head is pointing up,
both at the same time.

Because there is nothing under you,
you will weigh nothing.
You will float inside your no-spaceship.
The weight of the whole world
will press down on your ship.
Do not stay long.

Go straight ahead and begin
the long trip up.
Go 860 miles
through the inner core
and 1300 miles through
the outer core.
Drill up and up through the mantle.
And then through the magma,
and then through the crust,
and then through rocks
and sand and clay.
At last you will come to the surface.
You will be about 8000 miles
from where you started to dig
on the opposite side of the world.

If you started in the United States
you will come up at the bottom of the
Indian Ocean.
It will be delightfully cool,
but full of sharks.
Stay in your submarine
and steer it to the top.

93

There you can open the hatch.
You will see the sky and the sun.
Or perhaps it will be night
and you will see the moon and the stars.
If you have a sail
hoist it and start sailing home.
Or else paddle.
When you get home you can
tell everyone
you have dug the deepest hole
in the world
and are very, very glad
to be back on top of the earth.

Thinking About It

1 What was your favorite part of digging the hole? Why? Would you stop digging there? Tell your reasons.

2 You're going to be drilling for oil. How will you get to it? What will you dig through? How will you know if you've gone too far?

3 Plan tours or vacations through the earth. How could you get other people to go through the world instead of flying or sailing around it?

More About Our Changing Earth

Fiery volcanoes and folding rocks change the surface of our earth.

Discover what "old" means in Melvin Berger's book *As Old as the Hills*.

A DISCOVERING SCIENCE BOOK

AS OLD AS THE HILLS
by Melvin Berger
pictures by S.D. Schindler

95

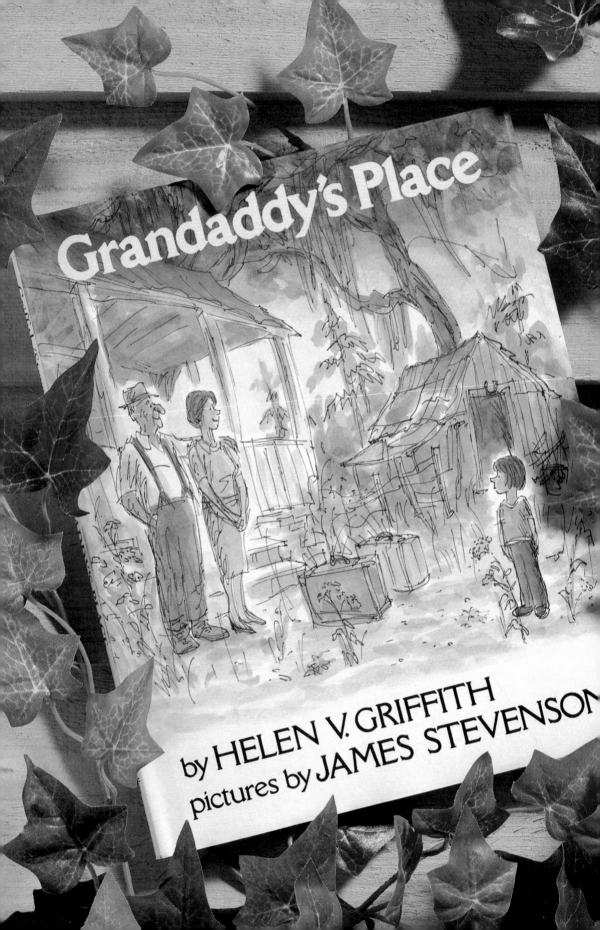

Grandaddy's Place

by HELEN V. GRIFFITH
pictures by JAMES STEVENSON

Chapter One

One day Momma said to Janetta, "It's time you knew your grandaddy." Momma and Janetta went to the railroad station and got on a train. Janetta had never ridden on a train before. It was a long ride, but she liked it. She liked hearing about Momma's growing-up days as they rode along. She didn't even mind sitting up all night.

But when they got to Grandaddy's place, Janetta didn't like it at all.

The house was old and small. The yard was mostly bare red dirt. There was a broken-down shed and a broken-down fence.

"I don't want to stay here," said Janetta.

Momma said, "This is where I grew up."

An old man came out onto the porch.

"Say hello to your grandaddy," Momma said. Janetta was too shy to say hello. "You hear me, Janetta?" Momma asked.

"Let her be," said Grandaddy.

So Momma just said, "Stay out here and play while I visit with your grandaddy."

They left Janetta standing on the porch. She didn't know
what to do. She had never been in the country before. She
thought she might sit on the porch, but there was a mean-
looking cat on the only chair. She thought she might sit on
the steps, but there was a wasps' nest up under the roof. The
wasps looked meaner than the cat. Some chickens were
taking a dust-bath in the yard. When Janetta came near, they
made mean sounds at her.

Janetta walked away. She watched the ground for bugs and snakes. All at once a giant animal came out of the broken-down shed. It came straight toward Janetta, and it was moving fast. Janetta turned and ran. She ran past the chickens and the wasps' nest and the mean-looking cat.

She ran into the house.

"There's a giant animal out there," she said.

Grandaddy looked surprised. "First I knew of it," he said.

"It has long legs and long ears and a real long nose," said Janetta.

Momma laughed. "Sounds like the mule," she said.

"Could be," said Grandaddy. "That mule's a tall mule."

"It chased me," said Janetta.

"It won't hurt you," Momma said. "Go back outside and make friends." But Janetta wouldn't go back outside.

"Nothing out there likes me," she said.

Chapter Two

After dark Momma and Grandaddy and Janetta sat out on the steps. The mean-looking cat wasn't anywhere around. Janetta hoped the wasps were asleep. She was beginning to feel sleepy herself. Then a terrible sound from the woods brought her wide awake.

"Was that the mule?" she asked.

"That was just an old hoot owl singing his song," said Grandaddy.

"It didn't sound like singing to me," said Janetta.

"If you were an owl, you'd be tapping your feet," said Grandaddy.

They sat and listened to the owl, and then Grandaddy said, "It was just this kind of night when the star fell into the yard."

"What star?" asked Janetta.

"Now, Daddy," said Momma.

"It's a fact," said Grandaddy. "It landed with a thump, and it looked all around, and it said, 'Where am I?'"

"You mean stars speak English?" asked Janetta.

"I guess they do," said Grandaddy, "because English is all I know, and I understood that star just fine."

"What did you say to the star?" asked Janetta.

Grandaddy said, "I told that star, 'You're in the United States of America,' and the star said, 'No, I mean what planet is this?' and I said, 'This is the planet Earth.'"

"Stop talking foolishness to that child," Momma said.

"What did the star say?" asked Janetta.

"The star said it didn't want to be on the planet Earth," said Grandaddy. "It said it wanted to get back up in the sky where it came from."

"So what did you do, Grandaddy?" Janetta asked.

"Nothing," said Grandaddy, "because just then the star saw my old mule."

"Was the star scared?" Janetta asked.

"Not a bit," said Grandaddy. "The star said, 'Can that mule jump?' and I said, 'Fair, for a mule,' and the star said, 'Good enough.' Then the star hopped up on the mule's back and said, 'Jump.'"

Momma said, "Now, you just stop that talk."

"Don't stop, Grandaddy," said Janetta.

"Well," Grandaddy said, "the mule jumped, and when they were high enough up the star hopped off and the mule came back down again."

"Was the mule all right?" asked Janetta.

"It was thoughtful for a few days, that's all," said Grandaddy.

Janetta stared up at the sky. "Which star was it, Grandaddy?" she asked.

"Now, Janetta," Momma said, "you know that's a made-up story."

Grandaddy looked up at the stars. "I used to know," he said, "but I'm not sure anymore."

"I bet the mule remembers," Janetta said.

"It very likely does," said Grandaddy.

From somewhere in the bushes some cats began to yowl. "That's just the worst sound I know," Momma said. "Janetta, chase those cats."

"They're just singing their songs," said Grandaddy.

"That's right, Momma," said Janetta. "If you were a cat, you'd be tapping your feet."

Momma laughed and shook her head. "One of you is as bad as the other," she said.

Chapter Three

The next day Grandaddy and Janetta went fishing. Janetta had never been fishing before. She didn't like it when Grandaddy put a worm on the hook.

"Doesn't that hurt him?" she asked.

"I'll ask him," said Grandaddy. He held the worm up in front of his face. "Worm, how do you feel about this hook?" he asked. He held the worm up to his ear and listened. Then he said to Janetta, "It's all right. That worm says there's nothing he'd rather do than fish."

"I want to hear him say that," Janetta said. She took the worm and held it up to her ear. "He's not saying anything," she said.

"That worm is shy," said Grandaddy. "But I know he just can't wait to go fishing." Grandaddy threw the line into the water. It wasn't long before he caught a fish. Then he gave Janetta the pole so that she could try. She threw the line in, and before long she had a fish, too. It was just a little fish. Janetta looked at it lying on the bank. It was moving its fins and opening and closing its mouth.

"I think it's trying to talk," Janetta said.

"It may be, at that," said Grandaddy. He held the fish up to his ear. "It says, 'Cook me with plenty of cornmeal,'" said Grandaddy.

"I want to hear it say that," said Janetta.

"Can you understand fish-talk?" asked Grandaddy.

"I don't know," said Janetta.

"Well, all that fish can talk is fish-talk," said Grandaddy.

Janetta held the fish up to her ear and listened. "It says, 'Throw me back,'" Janetta said.

Grandaddy looked surprised. "Is that a fact?" he asked.

"Clear as anything," said Janetta.

"Well, then I guess you'd better throw it back," said Grandaddy.

Janetta dropped the little fish into the water and watched it swim away. Grandaddy threw the line back in and began to fish again. "I never saw anybody learn fish-talk so fast," he said.

"I'm going to learn worm-talk next," said Janetta.

Chapter Four

When they had enough fish for supper, Janetta and
Grandaddy walked on home. The mean-looking cat came
running to meet them. He purred loud purrs and rubbed
against their legs.

"I didn't know that cat was friendly," Janetta said.

"He's friendly when you've been fishing," said Grandaddy.

The mule came out of the shed and walked toward them with its ears straight up. Janetta didn't know whether to run or not. The mule walked up to her and pushed her with its nose. Janetta was sorry she hadn't run.

"What do you know," Grandaddy said. "That old mule likes you."

"How can you tell?" Janetta asked.

"It only pushes you that way if it likes you," said Grandaddy.

"Really?" asked Janetta.

"It's a fact," said Grandaddy. "Up until now that mule has only pushed me and the cat and one of the chickens." Janetta was glad she hadn't run. She reached out her hand and touched the mule's nose.

"Grandaddy," she said, "what's the mule's name?"

"Never needed one," said Grandaddy. "It's the only mule around."

"Can I name it?" asked Janetta.

"You surely can," said Grandaddy.

Janetta thought. "I could call it Nosey," she said.

"That would suit that mule fine," said Grandaddy.

Janetta thought some more. "Maybe I'll call it Beauty," she said.

"That's a name I never would have thought of," said Grandaddy.

The mule gave Janetta another push. "This mule really likes me," Janetta said. "It must know I'm going to give it a name."

"You don't have to give it anything," said Grandaddy. "That mule just likes you for your own self."

108

Chapter Five

After supper Grandaddy and Momma and Janetta sat out on the steps and watched the night come on. The stars began to show themselves, one by one.

"Now I know what I'll name that mule," Janetta said. "I'll call it Star."

"Should have thought of that myself," said Grandaddy.

"Tomorrow I'll give the cat a name," said Janetta.

"Only fair, now the mule has one," said Grandaddy.

"After I get to know the chickens, I'll name them, too," said Janetta. "Then you'll be able to call them when you want them."

"That'll be handy," said Grandaddy.

"You'll be naming the hoot owl next," Momma said.

"I've been thinking about it," said Janetta.

Momma laughed, and Grandaddy did, too.

"Now, how did we get along around here before you came?" he asked.

"I've been wondering that, too, Grandaddy," said Janetta.

Helen V. Griffith
at age nine

I Was Janetta All Along

by Helen V. Griffith

Children often ask, "Where did you get the idea for your book?" It seems like a simple question, but it's not always easy to answer.

When I first wrote *Grandaddy's Place*, I thought I knew where the idea came from—a train trip I took to Florida when I was nine years old.

I loved riding in the train and watching the scenery change as we rode farther and farther south. My favorite sights were the shacks along the track with children playing around them.

It was early spring and every farmer seemed to be out plowing his field with the help of a big brown mule. To me it looked like the best possible way to live.

As the years passed, I often thought of that trip through the southern countryside. The setting of *Grandaddy's Place* comes from those memories, and for a while I thought the characters did, too. Then one day, when I was reading the story, I realized that I was Janetta and Grandaddy was my father.

I don't know why I didn't see that when I was writing the book. When I was young, my family spent summers on an old farm in Pennsylvania. My father worked on the railroad all day and then came home to hoe the truck patch (that's what we called our garden) and feed the pigs (we had eight). My father used to tell me stories about the conversations he had with those pigs, and he insisted that they were true. I kept saying, "Oh, Daddy, you're making it up," but I liked the stories.

We used to fish together, too, and sit on the porch after dark listening to the night sounds, just like Janetta and her grandaddy.

So when children ask me where my ideas come from I answer the question as well as I can. But sometimes I don't know the real answer yet myself.

Helen V. Griffith

Thinking About It

1

Of all the things Janetta did or saw while she was at Grandaddy's place, what was your favorite? What would you do if you could visit there?

2

You are Grandaddy. Find yourself in each picture during Janetta's visit and tell what you are thinking.

3

Janetta wants to send Grandaddy a present. What could she give him? Why is that gift a good idea?

The Knee-High Man

By Julius Lester

Retold as Reader's Theater by Caroline Feller Bauer

Illustrations by Kerry Marshall

Players

Narrator 1

Narrator 2

Knee-High Man

Mr. Horse

Mr. Bull

Mr. Owl

Narrator 1   Once upon a time there was a knee-high man. He was no taller than a person's knees. Because he was so short, he was very unhappy.

Narrator 2   He wanted to be big like everybody else.

Narrator 1   One day he decided to ask the biggest animal he could find how he could get big.

Narrator 2   He went to see Mr. Horse.

Knee-High Man   Mr. Horse, how can I get big like you?

Mr. Horse   Well, eat a whole lot of corn. Then run around a lot. After a while you'll be as big as me.

Narrator 1   The knee-high man did just that. He ate so much corn that his stomach hurt.

Knee-High Man   *(groan and hold stomach)*

Narrator 2   Then he ran and ran and ran until his legs hurt. But he didn't get any bigger.

Narrator 1   He decided that Mr. Horse had told him wrong. He decided to ask Mr. Bull.

Knee-High Man   Mr. Bull, how can I get big like you?

Mr. Bull   Eat a whole lot of grass. Then bellow as loud as you can. The first thing you know, you'll be big as me.

Narrator 2   So the knee-high man ate a whole field of grass. That made his stomach hurt.

Knee-High Man   *(groan and hold stomach)*

Narrator 1   He bellowed and bellowed and bellowed all day and all night. That made his throat hurt.

Narrator 2   But he didn't get any bigger. So he decided that Mr. Bull was all wrong, too.

Narrator 1   Now he didn't know anyone else to ask. One night he heard Mr. Owl hooting, and he remembered that Mr. Owl knew everything.

Knee-High Man   Mr. Owl, how can I get big like Mr. Horse and Mr. Bull?

Mr. Owl   What do you want to be big for?

Knee-High Man   I want to be big so that when I get into a fight, I can whip everybody.

Mr. Owl *(hooting)* Anybody ever try to pick a fight with you?

Narrator 1 The knee-high man thought a minute.

Knee-High Man Well, now that you mention it, nobody ever did try to start a fight with me.

Mr. Owl Well. You don't have any reason to fight. Therefore you don't have any reason to be bigger than you are.

Knee-High Man But Mr. Owl, I want to be big so I can see far into the distance.

Mr. Owl *(hooting)* If you climb a tall tree, you can see into the distance from the top.

Narrator 2 The knee-high man was quiet for a minute.

Knee-High Man Well, I hadn't thought of that.

Narrator 1 Mr. Owl hooted again.

Mr. Owl And that's what's wrong, Mr. Knee-High Man. You hadn't done any thinking at all. I'm smaller than you, and you don't see me worrying about being big. Mr. Knee-High Man, you wanted something that you didn't need.

Narrator 2 The End.

Pulling the Theme Together

Unexpected Situations

1 Knee-High Man would like to be taller. Is there anything you would like to change about yourself? What would Mr. Owl say to you about it?

2 Think about three of the characters in this book. What were some of the unexpected changes that happened to them? Would they say their changes were good? Why?

3 Think of something unexpected that might happen at school. How would your teacher and friends react? What would you do? How would it end up?

Books to Enjoy

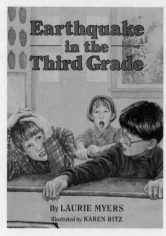

Earthquake in the Third Grade
by Laurie Myers
Clarion, 1993

Disaster strikes for John Jacobs when he knocks over his ant farm. Then he finds out his favorite teacher is moving. It's up to John and his friends to come up with a plan to keep Mrs. Lucas from leaving.

The Boy Who Didn't Believe in Spring
by Lucille Clifton
Illustrations by Brinton Turkle
Dutton, 1988

King Shabazz has heard enough about spring. "No such thing," he whispers in school. "Where's it at?" he hollers at home. Finally, he and his friend Tony search the neighborhood to see if they can find it.

Fossils Tell of Long Ago
written and illustrated by Aliki
HarperCollins, 1990

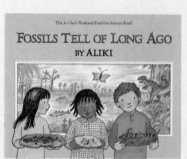

Fossils answer many questions about what our world was like long ago. This book explains how fossils were formed, what they can tell us, and where some fossils might be found.

On the Pampas
by Maria Cristina Brusca
Holt, 1991

When Maria leaves the city to vacation on her grandparents' estrancia, she begins a summer filled with adventure and excitement on the pampas.

The Magic School Bus
to the Center of the Earth
by Joanna Cole
Illustrations by Bruce Degen
Scholastic, 1987

All aboard as Ms. Frizzle's class takes a field trip you'll never forget. You won't believe the places you'll go in this magic bus!

Sunken Treasure
by Gail Gibbons
HarperCollins, 1988

Treasure Hunt! Hundreds of years ago ships filled with precious cargo sank to the bottom of the ocean. Today, treasure hunters go under the sea in search of gold and a peek into the past.

Literary Terms

Characters

Characters often change during a story. At the beginning of "The Ghost of Annabelle," Annabelle and Herbie don't like each other. By the end of the story, the author shows you that both Annabelle and Herbie have changed. Herbie thinks Annabelle makes a cute ghost. Annabelle says that Herbie has "a way with words."

Fiction

Stories that are created by an author are called **fiction.** What happens in "The Ghost of Annabelle" might seem real, but the author made this story up.

Nonfiction

Nonfiction is literature which gives facts. In *How to Dig a Hole to the Other Side of the World*, the author provides facts about what you would find if you traveled through the earth.

Rhyme

When the lines of a poem **rhyme**, the sounds
are repeated. Read aloud the first part of
Everett Anderson's Friend. Can you hear
the repeated sounds in *stay* and *13A?* What
other rhyming words can you hear?

Rhythm

Rhythm in a poem is a pattern of sounds.
When you read a poem that has rhythm,
you feel like moving your shoulders or feet
in time to it. Try reading "February" aloud
and notice how you say "Everett Anderson
in the snow." Can you feel the rhythm?

Setting

The **setting** in a story can make a character
think and feel a certain way. In
Grandaddy's Place, Janetta lives in the city,
but she goes to visit her grandfather, who
lives in the country. When she gets there,
she doesn't like the country at all. What
doesn't Janetta like about her grandfather's
farm? How does it make her feel?

Glossary

Words from your stories

al·ien (ā′lyən), a person who is not a citizen of the country in which he or she lives: *Aliens must register with the U.S. government when they arrive.* noun.

a·mount (ə mount′), a quantity or number of something: *No amount of coaxing would make the dog leave its owner.* noun.

a·part·ment (ə pärt′mənt), a room or group of rooms to live in; flat: *Our apartment is on the second floor.* noun.

as·bes·tos (as bes′təs), a mineral that does not burn. *noun.*

ash·es (ash′iz), what remains of a thing after it has thoroughly burned: *I removed the ashes from the fireplace.* noun plural.

bal·ance (bal′əns), to put or keep in a steady condition or position: *Can you balance a coin on its edge?* verb, **bal·anc·es, bal·anced, bal·anc·ing.**

balance

bur·row (bėr′ō), a hole dug in the ground by an animal for shelter or protection. *Rabbits live in burrows.* noun.

burrows

Cel·si·us (sel′sē əs). On the **Celsius thermometer,** 0 degrees is the temperature at which water freezes, and 100 degrees is the temperature at which water boils. *adjective.*

course (kôrs), a way; path; track; channel: *The explorers followed the course of the river.* noun.

cous·in (kuz′n), son or daughter of one's uncle or aunt. *My cousin is a teacher in India.* noun.

de·cide (di sīd′), to settle a question or dispute: *Fighting is not the best way to decide an argument.* verb, **de·cid·ed, de·cid·ing.**

a hat	**i** it	**oi** oil	**ch** child	**ə** stands for:
ā age	**ī** ice	**ou** out	**ng** long	a in about
ä far	**o** hot	**u** cup	**sh** she	e in taken
e let	**ō** open	**ú** put	**th** thin	i in pencil
ē equal	**ô** order	**ü** rule	**ᴛʜ** then	o in lemon
ėr term			**zh** measure	u in circus

dis·tance (dis′təns), a place far away: *She saw a light in the distance.* noun.

doom (düm), to sentence to an unhappy or terrible fate: *The prisoner was doomed to death.* verb.

e·nough (i nuf′), as much or as many as needed or wanted; sufficient: *Are there enough seats for all?* adjective.

far·ther (fär′ᴛʜər), to a greater distance: *We walked farther than we meant to.* adverb, comparative of **far.**

fig·ure (fig′yər), to think; consider: *I figured I should stop where I was.* verb. **fig·ures, fig·ured, fig·ur·ing.**

fo·reign·er (fôr′ə nər), a person from another country: *America is made up of foreigners from many lands.* noun.

gin·ger·ly (jin′jər lē), with extreme care: *Kelly walked gingerly across the ice.* adverb.

goo (gü), a thick, sticky substance: *Wear gloves so you don't get goo all over your hands.* noun.

gra·cious (grā′shəs), pleasant and kindly; courteous: *We were greeted in such a gracious manner that we immediately felt at ease.* adjective.

gra·cious·ly (grā′shəs lē), in a gracious manner: *The host and hostess served dinner graciously.* See **gracious.**

grump·y (grum′pē), bad-tempered; grouchy: *I went to bed late last night and woke up this morning feeling grumpy.* adjective, **grump·i·er, grump·i·est.**

guilt·y (gil′tē), deserving to be blamed and punished: *The jury found her guilty of theft.* adjective, **guilt·i·er, guilt·i·est.**

height (hīt), how tall a person is; how far up a thing goes: *Do you know your weight and height?* noun.

hoist (hoist), to raise on high; lift up, often with ropes and pulleys: *We hoisted the flag up the pole.* verb.

hys·ter·i·cal (hi ster′ə kəl), unnaturally excited: *Randy became hysterical when his dog got lost.* adjective.

in·sist (in sist′), to keep firmly to some demand, statement, or opinion: *He insists that he had a right to use his brother's tools.* verb.

125

in·va·sion (in vā′zhən), the act or fact of invading; entering by force or as an enemy; attack: *The small country prepared for an invasion by its enemy. noun.*

knock (nok), to hit and cause to fall: *The speeding car knocked over a sign. verb.*

lie (lī), to have one's body in a flat position along the ground or other surface: *We were lying in the grass looking at the stars. verb,* **lies, lay, lain, ly·ing.**

mag·nif·i·cent (mag nif′ə sənt), grand; stately; splendid: *From the palace we had a magnificent view of the mountains. adjective.*

a **magnificent** costume

men·tion (men′shən), to speak about: *I mentioned your idea to the group that is planning the picnic. verb.*

pleas·ant (plez′nt), that pleases; giving pleasure: *She usually took a pleasant swim on a hot day. adjective.*

pleas·ant·ly (plez′nt lē), in a pleasant manner: *He nodded pleasantly as we passed.* See **pleasant.**

pop·u·la·tion (pop′yə lā′shən), the number of people living in a place: *The population of the earth is over five billion. noun.*

rath·er (raŦH′ər), more willingly: *I would rather go today than tomorrow. adverb.*

rea·son (rē′zn), a cause; motive: *I have my reasons for doing it this way. noun.*

re·mark·a·ble (ri mär′kə bəl), worthy of notice; unusual: *He has a remarkable memory for names and faces. adjective.*

re·mem·ber (ri mem′bər), to call back to mind: *I can't remember that man's name. verb.*

rise (rīz), to go up; come up: *The kite rises in the air. verb,* **ris·es, rose, ris·en, ris·ing.**

rot (rot), to become rotten; decay; spoil: *So much rain will make the fruit rot. verb,* **rots, rot·ted, rot·ting.**

a hat	i it	oi oil	ch child	ə stands for:
ā age	ī ice	ou out	ng long	a in about
ä far	o hot	u cup	sh she	e in taken
e let	ō open	ù put	th thin	i in pencil
ē equal	ô order	ü rule	ŦH then	o in lemon
ėr term			zh measure	u in circus

stream (strēm), a flow of water in a channel or bed. Small rivers and large brooks are both called streams. *Because of the lack of rain many streams dried up. noun.*

stream

stub·born (stub′ərn), not giving in to argument or requests: *The stubborn boy refused to listen to reasons for not going out in the rain. adjective.*

sur·face (sėr′fis), the top of the ground or soil, or of a body of water or other liquid: *The stone sank beneath the surface of the water. noun.*

sur·round (sə round′), to shut in on all sides: *A high fence surrounds the field. verb.*

sur·vive (sər vīv′), to continue to live or exist; remain: *These cave paintings have survived for over 15,000 years. verb,* **sur·vives, sur·vived, sur·viv·ing.**

thought·ful (thôt′fəl), full of thought; thinking: *He is a very quiet and thoughtful person. adjective.*

throat (thrōt), the passage from the mouth to the stomach or the lungs: *A chicken bone got stuck in the dog's throat.*

un·der·stand (un′dər stand′), to get the meaning of: *Now I understand the teacher's question. verb,* **un·der·stands, un·der·stood, un·der·stand·ing.**

vol·ca·no (vol kā′nō), an opening in the earth's crust through which steam, ashes, and lava are sometimes forced out: *We climbed the side of the huge volcano. noun, plural* **vol·ca·noes** or **vol·ca·nos.**

volcano

vote (vōt), a formal expression of a choice about a proposal, a motion, or a candidate for office. *We took a vote on where to go for vacation. noun.*

127

Acknowledgments

Text

Pages 6–16: "The Ghost of Annabelle" from *What's the Matter with Herbie Jones?* by Suzy Kline. Text © 1986 by Suzy Kline. Reprinted by permission of G.P. Putnam's Sons.

Pages 18–32: From *Company's Coming* by Arthur Yorinks, illustrated by David Small. Text copyright © 1988 by Arthur Yorinks. Illustrations copyright © 1988 by David Small. Reprinted by permission of Crown Publishers, Inc.

Pages 34–38: "Kan Kan Can" by Carmen Tafolla. Copyright © 1991 by Carmen Tafolla.

Pages 40–49: *Everett Anderson's Friend* by Lucille Clifton. Copyright © 1976 by Lucille Clifton. First appeared in *Everett Anderson's Friend* published by Holt, Rinehart, and Winston. Reprinted by permission of Curtis Brown, Ltd.

Pages 50–53: From *Everett Anderson's Year* by Lucille Clifton. Copyright © 1974 by Lucille Clifton. First appeared in *Everett Anderson's Year* published by Holt, Rinehart, and Winston. Reprinted by permission of Curtis Brown, Ltd.

Pages 54–56: From "Profile: Lucille Clifton" by Rudine Sims Bishop, *Language Arts,* February, 1982. Copyright © 1982 by the National Council of Teachers of English. Reprinted by permission.

Pages 54–56: "Everett Anderson's Author" by Lucille Clifton. Copyright © 1991 by Lucille Clifton.

Pages 58–59: "Digging Up the Past" by Emily Schell, *U*S* Kids,* April, 1989, pages 36–37. Copyright © 1989 by Weekly Reader Corporation. Reprinted by special permission granted by *U*S* Kids,* published by Weekly Reader Corporation.

Pages 60–76: *The House on Maple Street* by Bonnie Pryor. Text copyright © 1987 by Bonnie Pryor. Reprinted by permission of William Morrow and Company, Inc.

Pages 78–94: *How to Dig a Hole to the Other Side of the World* by Faith McNulty. Text copyright © 1979 by Faith McNulty. Reprinted by permission of HarperCollins Publishers.

Pages 96–109: From *Grandaddy's Place* by Helen V. Griffith, illustrations by James Stevenson. Copyright © 1987 by Helen V. Griffith. Illustration copyright © 1987 by James Stevenson. Reprinted by permission of Greenwillow Books, a division of William Morrow & Company, Inc.

Pages 110–112: "I Was Janetta All Along" by Helen V. Griffith. Copyright © 1991 by Helen V. Griffith.

Pages 114–118: "The Knee-High Man" from *The Knee-High Man and Other Tales* by Julius Lester. Copyright © 1972 by Julius Lester. Used by permission of Dial Books for Young Readers.

Artists

Flora Jew, cover, 1-3

Third-grade classes, Pritzker School and LaSalle Language Academy, Chicago, Illinois, 6–17, 122

David Small, 4, 18–33

Eve Olitsky, 34–39

Gil Ashby, 4, 40–53, 55, 57, 123

Larry McEntire, 60–77

Kathy Petrauskas, 5, 78–94, 122

James Stevenson, 5, 96–109, 110, 113

Photographs

Page 54: Courtesy of St. Mary's College of Maryland, Copyright © Layle Silbert.

Pages 58–59: William Sallaz

Page 110: Courtesy of Helen V. Griffith

Page 124T: Soil Conservation Service/U.S. Dept. of Agriculture

Page 126: Carlton C. McAvery

Page 127T: Don and Pat Valenti

Page 127B: Hugo Brehme/Rapho/Photo Researchers

Glossary

The contents of the Glossary have been adapted from *Beginning Dictionary,* Copyright © 1988, Scott, Foresman and Company.